MEMORY GAMES for Clever Kids

Buster Books

Puzzles and solutions
by Dr Gareth Moore

B.Sc (Hons) M.Phil Ph.D

Illustrations and cover artwork by Chris Dickason

Designed by Zoe Bradley
Edited by Emma Taylor
Cover design by Angie Allison

First published in Great Britain in 2022 by Buster Books,
an imprint of Michael O'Mara Books Limited,
9 Lion Yard, Tremadoc Road, London SW4 7NQ

W www.mombooks.com/buster

f Buster Books

🐦 @BusterBooks

📷 @buster_books

Puzzles and solutions © Gareth Moore 2022

Illustrations and layouts © Buster Books 2022

A CIP catalogue record for this book is available from the British Library.

ISBN: 978-1-78055-872-1

2 4 6 8 10 9 7 5 3 1

Papers used by Buster Books are natural, recyclable products made of wood from
well-managed, FSC®-certified forests and other controlled sources. The manufacturing
processes conform to the environmental regulations of the country of origin.

Printed and bound in July 2022 by CPI Group (UK) Ltd,
108 Beddington Lane, Croydon, CR0 4YY, United Kingdom

INTRODUCTION

Get ready to push your recall skills to the limit in this
fun-filled book that's packed full of memory games.

The puzzles are arranged so that they get more difficult
as you work your way through the book, so start at
the beginning to get warmed up before moving
on to the trickier puzzles.

First, read the instructions that go with each memory game.
On some of the pages, there is more than one puzzle, but if so
you only need to try to remember one of them at a time. After
you turn the page to do the recall part of the game, the book
will then tell you when to turn back for the second puzzle.

It's also a good idea to write and draw in pencil,
so that you can rub your answers out if they're
not quite right (and then try again).

Good luck and have fun!

Take a good look at each of the children below. When you're ready, turn the page and follow the instructions.

Here are the same five children, but two of them have swapped places. Can you circle the two that have moved?

Look closely at these four socks and think of a way of describing the pattern on each of them. Once you think you will remember the patterns, turn the page.

Two of the socks have gone missing.
Can you describe them both?

Sock 1: ....

Sock 2: ....

Look closely at these four smileys, and try to remember the faces that they're pulling. Once you think you won't forget them, turn the page.

Two of the faces are now blank. Can you draw them back in?

Study this list of sports for as long as you need to memorize it. Once you're ready, turn the page and follow the instructions.

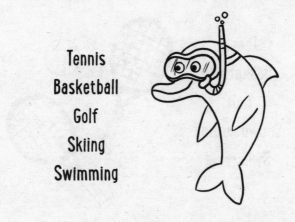

Tennis
Basketball
Golf
Skiing
Swimming

Now try again with this list, then turn the page once you're ready:

Hockey
Baseball
Football
Badminton
Running

One of the sports has changed. Can you circle the new entry?

Tennis
Basketball
Golf
Snowboarding
Swimming

Once you've found the new entry, turn back and try again with the second list of sports.

Can you circle the sport which has changed?

Hockey
Basketball
Football
Badminton
Running

Can you help these aliens remember their routes home?
Take a look at path 1 and then, once you feel confident you'll
remember it, turn the page and see if you can redraw it.

1)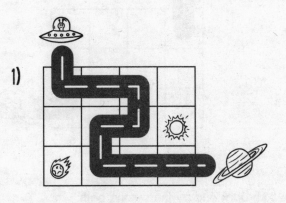

Once you've redrawn the previous path, try with this path, too:

2)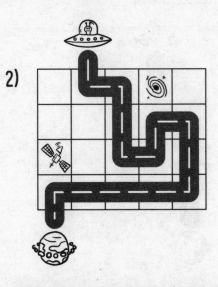

Draw in the missing parts of the alien's path home:

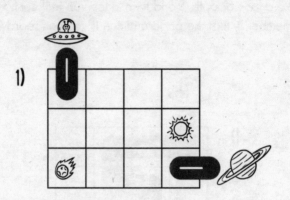

1)

Now turn back and try the second path.

Draw in the missing parts of the alien's path home:

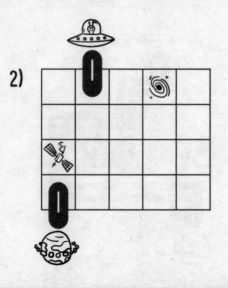

2)

Have a good look at the following fruit platter, and try to remember what's on it and where. On the following page the same picture will appear, but with five differences. Once you think you'll remember the picture below well enough to know what's changed, turn the page.

Circle the five differences in the image below:

Have a good look at the following treasure map and try to memorize the route from START to FINISH. When you're ready, turn the page and see if you can redraw it.

Here's the same map, but without the route marked.
Can you draw it back in?

Look closely at these four flowers. Once you think you'll remember what each one looks like, turn the page.

One of the flowers has been replaced by a new flower.
Can you circle it?

Take a good look at this set of five facts about six dinosaurs. Spend as long as you feel you need to memorize them, then turn the page and answer the questions. The list of dinosaur names will be given again.

Argentinosaurus
Diplodocus
Stegosaurus
Triceratops
Tyrannosaurus
Velociraptor

- The name 'velociraptor' means 'speedy thief'.

- Stegosaurus and tyrannosaurus dinosaurs did not exist at the same time – they were separated by about 80 million years.

- Argentinosaurus is one of the largest dinosaurs ever discovered.

- A triceratops had three horns on its face.

- The diplodocus had a very long neck, which was about seven metres long – that's more than three times as long as a giraffe's neck!

MEMORY GAME 9 →

Use the following dinosaurs to answer the questions below:

Argentinosaurus
Diplodocus
Stegosaurus
Triceratops
Tyrannosaurus
Velociraptor

1) What type of dinosaur had three horns on its face?

....

2) Which dinosaur had a neck measuring about seven metres in length?

....

3) Which dinosaur has a name that means 'speedy thief'?

....

4) Which of these dinosaurs is one of the largest ever discovered?

....

5) Which two of these dinosaurs lived 80 million years apart, according to the previous page?

....and

....

Take a look at the item below, then turn the page and see if you can redraw the missing parts.

Here's the same picture, but with some of the features removed.
Can you draw them all back in?

Once you're done, check back and see how your version
compares to the original.

Take a good look at these six people who are on their way to work. Then, once you think you'll remember what you've seen, turn the page.

It's getting busy! Circle the two new people who have joined the crowd.

Take a look at these four shapes, then turn the page and see if you can redraw them all - and in the same order.

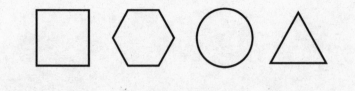

Now try the same again with the following new list of shapes - although this time there is no need to remember the order they were in:

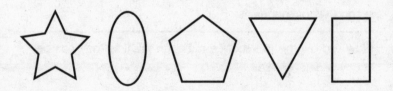

Redraw the four shapes, in the same order as on the previous page:

Once you have done this, turn back a page and try the second set of shapes.

Now redraw the five shapes, although this time they can be in any order you like:

Take a look at the following clothes, and try to remember what's where. Once you think you'll remember, turn the page.

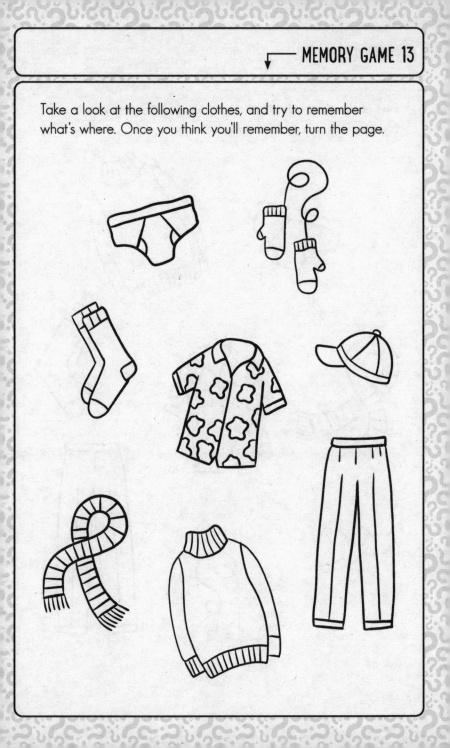

Five of the items have changed places. Circle the three items of clothing which *haven't* moved.

Have a good look at this map of South America, and in particular where the six listed countries are located. Once you think you'll remember where they all are, turn the page and follow the instructions.

Can you identify each of the six labelled countries?
The names of the six countries are given below.

Argentina Brazil Chile Colombia Uruguay Venezuela

Take a look at this simple picture, then turn the page and see how accurately you can redraw it.

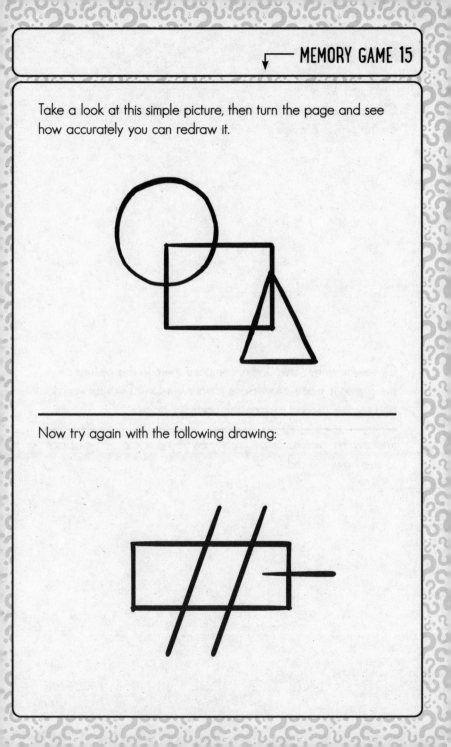

Now try again with the following drawing:

Can you now draw the shapes, exactly as they were arranged on the previous page?

Once you've redrawn them, compare them to the picture on the previous page. How close is your version? Then turn back and try the second task on the previous page.

Redraw the picture as accurately as you can, then check back to see how you did.

Study the picture below and try to learn the name of each of the five dancers. Once you're done, turn the page and follow the instructions.

Two of the dancers have had their names swapped.
Can you circle the two names which have changed places?

Ashley

James

Jordan

Seetha

Luke

Take a minute to memorize these five items of pirate treasure, paying particular attention to the order they are written in. When you're ready, turn the page and follow the instructions.

1) Coins
2) Tiara
3) Sword
4) Pearls
5) Diamonds

Now try again with these further five treasures. Turn the page once you're ready – but be careful, since this time you won't be given the items to choose from!

1) Gold
2) Skeleton key
3) Rubies
4) Goblet
5) Shield

Can you now rewrite the five treasures in the same order as on the previous page? The items are given below to help, but three extra items have been added to make it trickier.

1) ....

2) ....

3) ....

4) ....

5) ....

Coins	Crown	Diamonds	Map	Necklace
	Pearls	Sword	Tiara	

Once you've written in the objects, turn back and try the second list of treasures.

Can you write down all five pirate treasures in the same order as on the previous page?

1) ....

2) ....

3) ....

4) ....

5) ....

Some of the squares in this picture have been shaded in.
On the next page you'll see the same picture, but all of the
squares will be blank. It will be your job to shade them in to
match this page.

Spend as long as you think you need in order to remember
which squares are shaded, then turn the page.

Now do the same with this second pattern:

Shade the squares to match the picture on the previous page:

1)

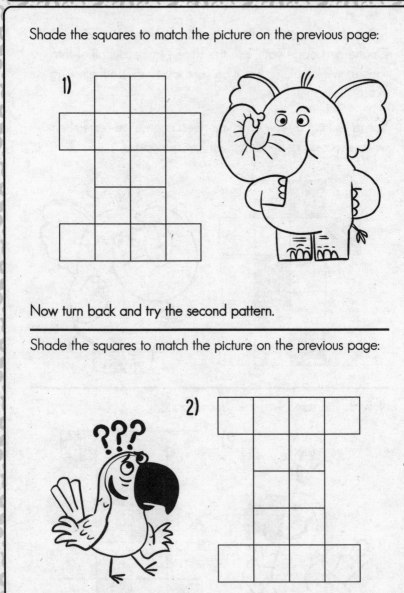

Now turn back and try the second pattern.

Shade the squares to match the picture on the previous page:

2)

Take a look at the following face, and in particular the eyes, nose and mouth. Once you think you'll remember them, turn the page.

By picking from the various options below, can you redraw the face exactly as it appeared on the previous page? Once done, compare back to the original picture.

Take a good look at these four delicious cupcakes. Once you think you'll remember them all, turn the page.

Two new cupcakes have been added. Can you circle both of them?

Spend a minute or two studying this list of European countries and their capital cities, until you think you will remember them all. Then, turn the page and follow the instructions.

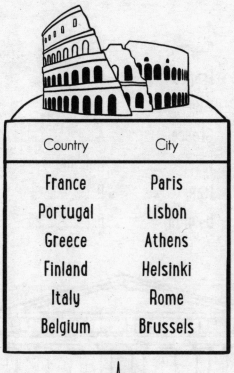

Country	City
France	Paris
Portugal	Lisbon
Greece	Athens
Finland	Helsinki
Italy	Rome
Belgium	Brussels

Now see if you can fill in all of the blanks with the names of either the corresponding country or capital city. The first letter of each is given:

Country	City
France	P...................
P...................	Lisbon
Greece	A...................
F...................	Helsinki
Italy	R...................
Belgium	B...................

You're going to the shop to buy a few groceries and decide to learn the list instead of simply writing it down.

Memorize the following list of items to buy, then turn the page once you're ready:

Bananas
Eggs
Milk
Cheese
Pet food
Apples
Magazine
Orange juice

Can you remember the shopping list, and write it down below?
The first letter of each item has been given to help you.

B.............................

E.............................

M.............................

C.............................

P.............................

A.............................

M.............................

O.............................

Spend up to a minute trying to memorize the list of musical instruments below. Then, turn the page and follow the instructions.

Piano
Guitar
Drums
Flute
Violin

Now try again with this new set of instruments, turning the page once ready:

Trumpet
Clarinet
Saxophone
Keyboard
Trombone

Can you write the missing instruments back on to the two blank lines?

Piano

....

Drums

....

Violin

Then turn back to the previous page and try the second list.

Can you write in the three missing instruments?

....

Clarinet

....

Keyboard

....

Take a good look at these six athletes for about a minute. Then, turn the page and follow the instructions.

Two of the athletes have left. Can you say which sports they were playing?

Missing sport 1: ....

Missing sport 2: ....

Have a good look at the following picture, and try to remember what it looks like. On the following page the same picture will appear, but with five differences. Once you think you'll remember the picture below well enough to know what's changed, turn the page.

Circle the five differences in the image below:

Five objects have been left in five different rooms as shown on this plan. Memorize which object is in each room, then turn the page.

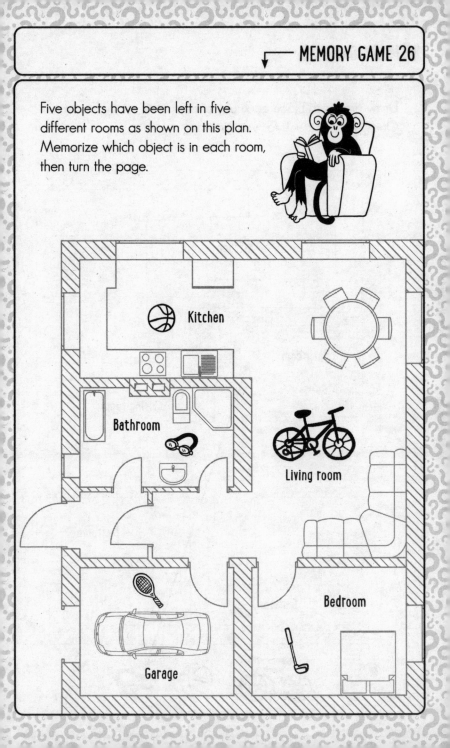

Kitchen

Bathroom

Living room

Garage

Bedroom

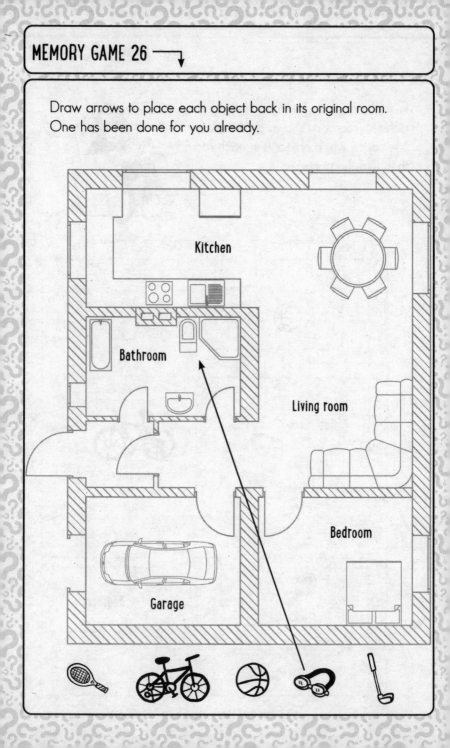

MEMORY GAME 26 →

Draw arrows to place each object back in its original room.
One has been done for you already.

Spend a minute or so learning the names of these pets. When time is up, turn the page and follow the instructions.

Fluffy

Harry

Fifi

Milo

Daisy

Bruce

Here are the same animals again, but in a different order and without their names. Can you complete each name label?

....

....

....

....

....

....

Some of the squares in this picture have been shaded in. On the next page you'll see the same picture, but all of the squares will be blank. It will be your job to shade them in to match this page.

Spend as long as you think you need in order to remember which squares are shaded, then turn the page.

1)

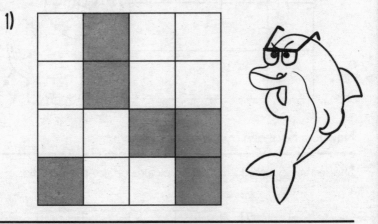

Now do the same with this second pattern:

2)

Shade the squares to match the picture on the previous page:

1)

Now turn back and try the second pattern.

Shade the squares to match the picture on the previous page:

2)

Spend a minute looking at these balloons, and try to remember the set of five numbers printed on them. You don't need to remember what order they're in. Then, once you're ready, turn the page and follow the instructions.

Now try remembering these six numbers:

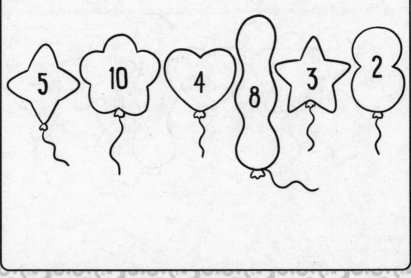

Can you write the same five numbers back on to these blank balloons? They can be in any order you like:

Once you've written a number on each of the balloons, turn back a page and try the second set of numbers.

Can you rewrite all six numbers on to these blank balloons?:

Have a good look at the following journey, shown by the dashed line. When you're ready, turn the page and see if you can redraw it.

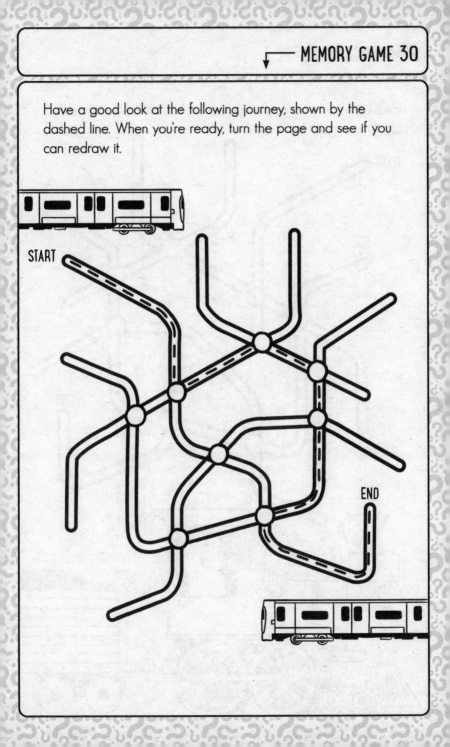

Here's the same transport map, but without the route marked! Can you draw it back in?

START

END

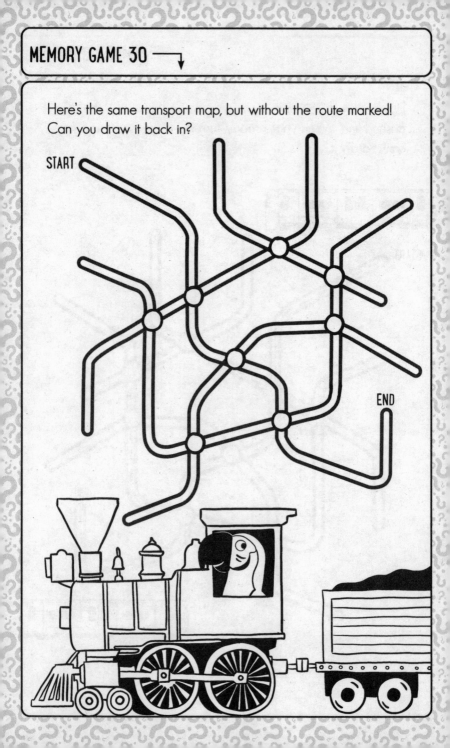

Study these six items of cutlery until you think you'll remember what you've seen. When you're ready, turn the page.

Two new items of cutlery have been added to the group.
Can you circle them both?

Take a look at the following face, and in particular the eyes, nose, mouth and ears. Once you think you'll remember them, turn the page.

By picking from the various options below, can you redraw the face exactly as it appeared on the previous page? Once done, compare back to the original picture!

Spend one or two minutes studying this list of facts about African countries, or until you think you have memorized them. Then, turn the page and follow the instructions.

- The largest African country by area is Algeria.

- The highest African mountain is Mount Kilimanjaro, which is in Tanzania.

- The capital of Egypt is Cairo.

- South Africa is the southernmost African country (which means it's the furthest south).

- The equator passes through several African countries, including Kenya.

Fill in the gaps with the missing countries from the previous page - but be careful, since the facts are in a different order.

If you find this too hard, the list of countries you need is written upside down at the bottom of this page.

1) The highest African mountain is Mount Kilimanjaro, which

   is in ....

2) The capital of .... is Cairo.

3) The equator passes through several African countries,

   including ....

4) The largest African country by area is ....

5) .... is the southernmost African country.

Algeria   Egypt   Kenya   South Africa   Tanzania

Can you identify all six of the animals on this page? Once you think that you'll remember where each animal is and what direction it is facing, turn to the next page.

Three of the animals have moved position or changed direction. Can you circle the three that have changed?

Can you help these squirrels remember their routes home?
Take a look at path 1 and then, once you feel confident you'll
remember it, turn the page and see if you can redraw it.

1)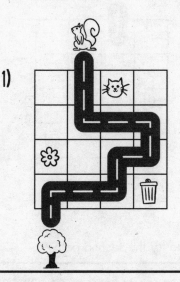

Once you've redrawn the previous path, try with this path, too:

2)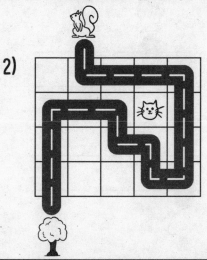

Draw in the missing parts of the squirrel's path home:

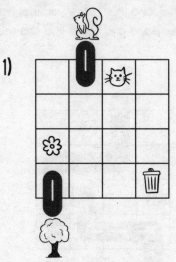

1)

Now turn back and try the second path.

Draw in the missing parts of the squirrel's path home:

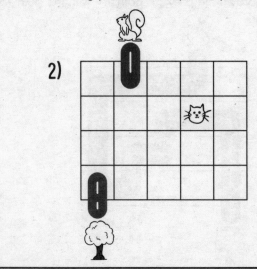

2)

Each of these household devices has been given a friendly name. Spend a minute or two learning the name of each device, then turn the page and follow the instructions.

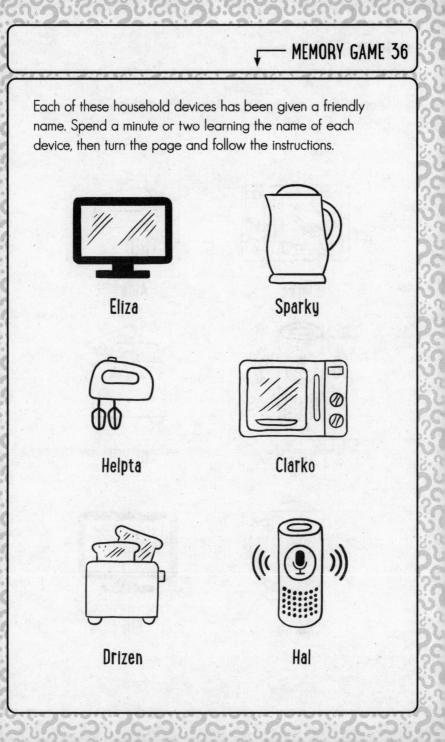

Eliza

Sparky

Helpta

Clarko

Drizen

Hal

Some of these devices have changed their names. Can you circle all of the new names?

Clarko

Aida

Dave

Drizen

Parky

Eliza

Take a look at the following pieces of sporting equipment, and try to remember what's where. Once you think you'll remember, turn the page.

Four of the items have changed places. Circle the four items of sporting equipment which *haven't* moved.

Take a look at this collection of items on a lost-property stand.
Once you think you will remember them all, turn the page.

Some of the items have now been collected. Can you write down descriptions of the three items that are now gone?

Describe the items here:

1) ....

2) ....

3) ....

Have a good look at the following picture, and try to remember what it looks like. On the next page the same picture will appear, but with five differences. Once you think you'll remember the picture below well enough to know what's changed, turn the page.

Circle the five differences in the image below:

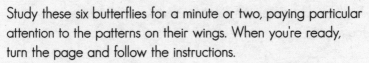

Study these six butterflies for a minute or two, paying particular attention to the patterns on their wings. When you're ready, turn the page and follow the instructions.

Two new butterflies have just landed. Can you circle them both?

Take a look at the following picture, then turn the page and see if you can redraw the missing parts.

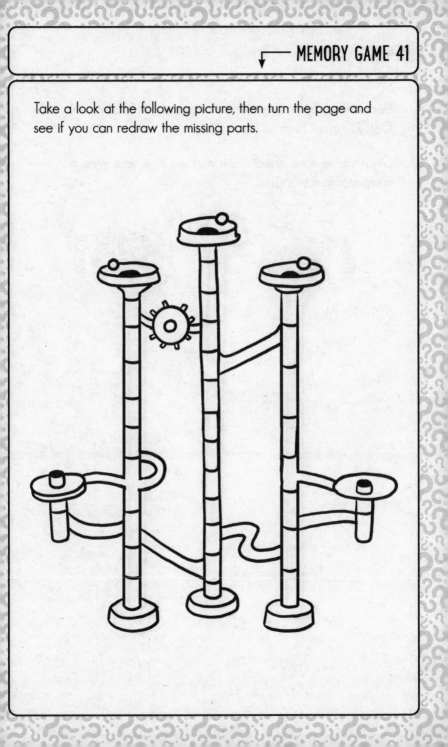

Here's the same picture, but with some of the features removed. Can you draw them all back in?

Once you're done, check back and see how your version compares to the original.

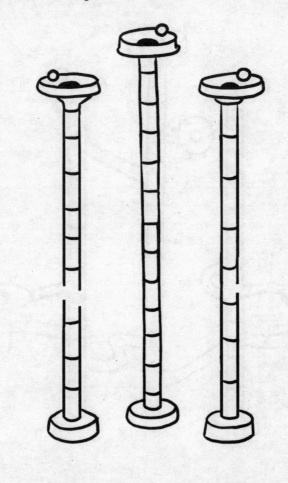

Have you ever had to remember a password or a PIN code? Try memorizing these two made-up codes, then turn the page and see if you can remember them.

House alarm code:

1423

Library account password:

BooksRGreat

Now try remembering this trickier password and code. Turn the page once you're ready, and see if you can recall them.

Email password:

CoMpUtErPaSs

Bike-lock code:

246810

Can you fill in the correct code and password below?

House alarm code: ....

Library account password: ....

Now turn back a page and try again with the other codes and passwords.

Can you complete the missing information?

Email password: ....

Bike-lock code: ....

Spend a few minutes learning these six facts about animals. Then, once you're ready, turn the page and see if you can answer the questions.

- Owls are nocturnal animals, which means they are active at night and sleep during the day.

- Emperor penguins are the largest type of penguin, and are much bigger than you might expect – they grow to about one metre tall.

- The spots on leopards are known as 'rosettes', which is because they resemble the shape of a rose.

- Flamingos are born grey or white, but turn pink during the first couple of years of their life.

- Blue whales are the largest animals that have ever existed – even bigger than the dinosaurs were!

- Komodo dragons are giant, poisonous lizards which can be found in the country of Indonesia – and they can grow up to three metres long!

Can you answer the questions below?

1) What is the largest type of penguin?

....

2) In which country can Komodo dragons be found in the wild?

....

3) What type of bird turns pink a couple of years after it is born?

....

4) What name is given to the spots on a leopard, due to their resemblance to the shape of a rose?

....

5) What do you call an animal that is active at night and asleep during the day, such as an owl?

....

6) What is the largest type of animal ever to exist?

....

It's time to go shopping again, and the list of items you need to buy is listed below. Study the shopping list for about a minute. Then, turn the page and follow the instructions.

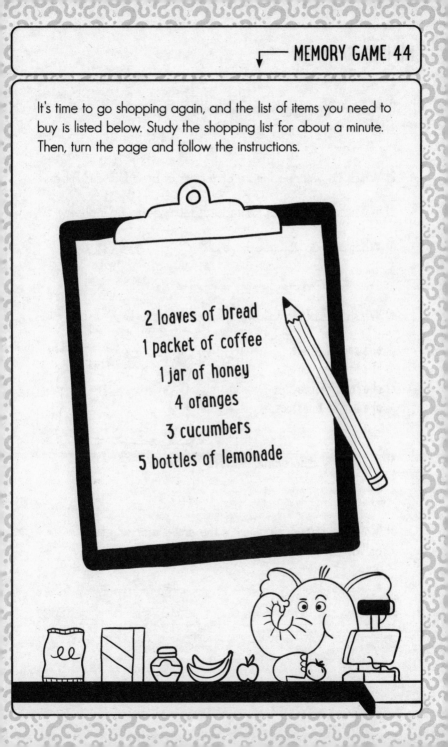

2 loaves of bread
1 packet of coffee
1 jar of honey
4 oranges
3 cucumbers
5 bottles of lemonade

1) How many oranges do you need to buy?

....

2) Which do you need more of: loaves of bread, or cucumbers?

....

3) What item do you need five of?

....

4) Which one of the following do you need to buy?

   a) a packet of tea
   b) a bag of onions
   c) a jar of honey
   d) a box of tomatoes

5) How many different items were on the list?

....

6) Now write down as much of the entire shopping list
   as you can recall:

....

....

....

....

Look closely at these six cakes. Once you think you'll remember what each one looks like, turn the page.

Two of the birthday cakes have swapped places. Can you circle the two which have been swapped?

Each of the following countries has a capital city which shares exactly the same name. For example, the capital of Luxembourg (the country) is Luxembourg (the city).

Memorize the names of these six countries – and how to spell them – as well as you can, then turn the page.

DJIBOUTI
LUXEMBOURG
MONACO
SAN MARINO
SINGAPORE
VATICAN CITY

Can you write down the names of the six countries? Half of the letters from each name have been given to you as a clue.

D_I_O_T_

L_X_M_O_R_

M_N_C_

S_N M_R_N_

S_N_A_O_E

V_T_C_N C_T_

Take a look at this simple picture, then turn the page and see how accurately you can redraw it.

Now try again with the following drawing:

Can you now draw the crown exactly as it was shown on the previous page?

Once you've drawn the crown, compare it to the one on the previous page. How close is your version?

After you've compared the images, try the second task on the previous page.

Redraw the treasure chest as accurately as you can, then check back to see how you did.

Take some time to remember the three numbers below, then turn the page and answer the two maths questions. Try to do this without writing down the three numbers again.

5 8 10

Now try memorizing these three numbers instead, and again then turn the page and answer the questions.

7 11 15

1) What number do you get if you add together the two lowest values?

....

2) Which of these three totals can you form by adding together any two of the numbers?

   a) 14   b) 16   c) 18

Once you have answered the questions, turn back a page and try the second set of numbers.

---

1) Which of these three totals can you form by adding together any two of the numbers?

   a) 16   b) 18   c) 20

2) What number do you get if you subtract the lowest number from the highest number?

....

Spend up to a minute trying to memorize the list of words beginning with 'L' below. Then, turn the page and follow the instructions.

Letter

Lion

Lime

Lemon

Ladder

Now try again with this new set of 'L' words, turning the page once ready:

Lamb

Laptop

Log

Lettuce

Lizard

Can you write the missing 'L' words back on to the two blank lines?

Letter

....

Lime

....

Ladder

Then turn back to the previous page and try the second list.

Can you write in the three missing 'L' words?

....

Laptop

....

Lettuce

....

Read this recipe for making a salad, and try to remember the ingredients and instructions as best you can. Once you think you're ready, turn the page and answer the questions.

Ingredients:

- Lettuce
- Tomatoes
- Mozzarella cheese
- Olive oil
- Basil leaves

Instructions:

1) Wash the lettuce leaves and add to a bowl

2) Chop the tomatoes into quarters and place on top of the lettuce

3) Tear some mozzarella cheese and add on top

4) Pour a small amount of olive oil into the bowl, and give everything a stir

5) Add some basil leaves on top of the salad – and enjoy!

1) How many numbered steps were there in the instructions?

....

2) What instruction was given for preparing the tomatoes?

   a) Cut the tomatoes into halves
   b) Mash up the tomatoes
   c) Add the tomatoes whole
   d) Chop the tomatoes into quarters

3) What kind of cheese did the recipe require?

....

4) One of the steps said to add olive oil – and then do what?

....

5) What is the final ingredient added to the salad?

....

6) Which ingredient has not been mentioned in the previous five questions, either in the question or as the answer?

....

Take a look at the following illustration, then turn the page and see if you can redraw the missing parts.

Here's the same picture, but with some of the features removed. Can you draw them all back in?

Once you're done, check back and see how your version compares to the original.

Six objects have been left behind in this playground. Take a look at what's lying where. Then, once you think you'll remember this, turn the page and continue.

Draw arrows to place each item back in its original position.
One is done for you already.

Look closely at these seven robots, then turn the page once you're happy you'll remember what each one looks like.

Four of the robots have been replaced by new ones! Can you circle all of the new robots?

Take a look at this simple picture, then turn the page and see how accurately you can redraw it.

Now try again with the following drawing:

Can you now redraw the picture, exactly as it was shown on the previous page?

Once you've redrawn it, compare back to the picture on the previous page. How close is your version? Then turn back and try the second task on the previous page.

Redraw the picture as accurately as you can, then check back to see how you did.

Study this set of dominoes for a minute, and try to memorize exactly what each domino looks like. Then, turn the page and follow the instructions.

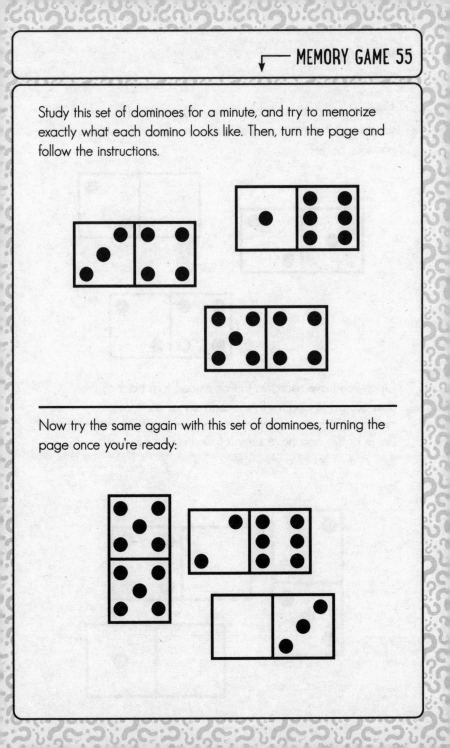

Now try the same again with this set of dominoes, turning the page once you're ready:

Some of the dots have been erased from the dominoes. Can you restore this picture so it exactly matches the image on the previous page?

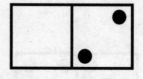

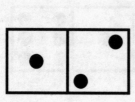

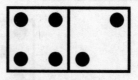

Once you have redrawn the dominoes, turn back to the previous page and try the second set of dominoes.

Some of the dots have been erased again. Can you redraw the original set of dominoes?

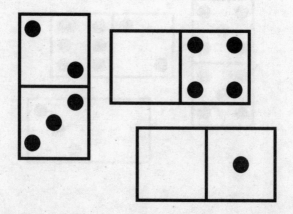

Study these six aliens for a minute or so, and try to memorize each of their names. When time is up, turn the page and follow the instructions.

Zook

Ringo

Babble

Dolly

Fizz

Marta

The aliens have all moved around! Can you write the correct name under each alien?

....

....

....

....

....

....

Have a good look at the following picture, and try to remember what it looks like. On the next page the same picture will appear, but with five differences. Once you think you'll remember the picture below well enough to know what's changed, turn the page.

Circle the five differences in the image below:

Take a look at these six shapes, and the order they are in. On the next page you will be shown the shapes again and asked to put them into the same order as below. Once you think you're ready to do this, turn the page.

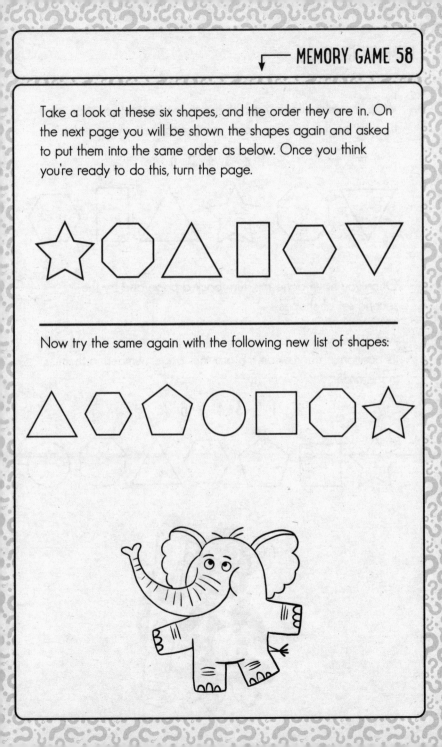

Now try the same again with the following new list of shapes:

Write a number inside each shape to represent its position in the row on the previous page, numbering them in this order:

1 2 3 4 5 6

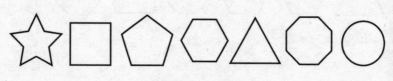

Once you have done this, turn back a page and try the second set of shapes.

As before, now write a number inside each shape to represent its position in the row on the previous page, numbering them in this order:

1 2 3 4 5 6 7

Spend a couple of minutes reading these facts about various capital cities. Once time's up, turn the page and follow the instructions.

- The capital of Australia is Canberra.

- Some countries have two capital cities. For example, Bolivia's capitals are Sucre and La Paz.

- Nauru, a tiny island to the northeast of Australia, is the only country in the world which does not have an official capital city.

- Rio de Janeiro was once the capital city of Brazil, but now the capital is Brasília.

- New York City is the largest city (in terms of the number of people living there) in the United States (US), but the US capital is Washington, D.C.

1) Which is the only country not to have an official capital city?

....

2) Which country has the two capital cities of Sucre and Le Paz?

   a) Brazil
   b) Benin
   c) Bolivia
   d) Belgium

3) What is the name of the capital of Australia?

....

4) Which city is the current capital of Brazil?

   a) Washington DC
   b) Rio de Janeiro
   c) London
   d) Brasília

5) True or false: New York City is the capital city of the United States.

   a) True
   b) False

Study this list of words beginning with 'b' for about a minute.
Then, turn the page and follow the instructions.

Banana
Brainteaser
Baby
Bicycle
Bat
Blue

The six words from the previous page are listed below along with four extra words, and not in the same order. However, to make it trickier, all of the words have been written backwards. Can you circle the four new words?

ananaB

nworB

resaetniarB

kcalB

eulB

taB

elcyciB

niarB

taoB

ybaB

Look closely at these five smileys. Once you think you won't forget them, turn the page - where you'll be asked to redraw them all.

Can you redraw the five smileys in these empty circles?

Study these seven monsters for about a minute. Then, turn the page and follow the instructions.

The monsters have all moved around and two new monsters have joined the group. Can you circle them both?

Try to remember the name of each of these eight people. Then, once you think you're ready, turn the page and see if you can answer the recall question.

Hannah

Ben

Richard

Jayne

Edward

Chloe

Kaiya

Dallas

Each of the people has swapped their name with another person. Can you draw lines to join them into the four pairs who have exchanged names?

Hannah

Chloe

Kaiya

Jayne

Richard

Edward

Dallas

Ben

Can you help these bees remember their routes home? Take a look at path 1 and then, once you feel confident you'll remember it, turn the page and see if you can redraw it.

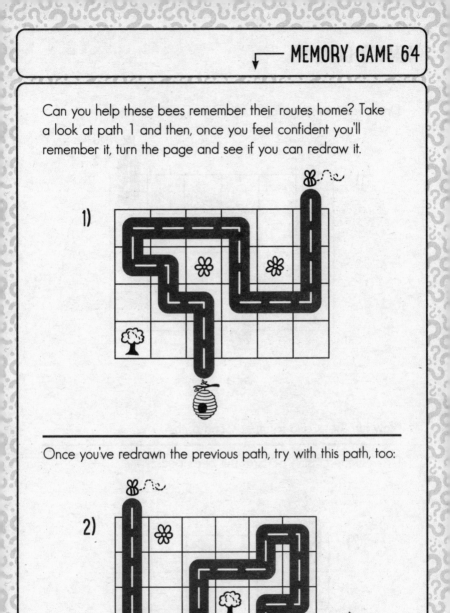

1)

Once you've redrawn the previous path, try with this path, too:

2)

Draw in the missing parts of the bee's path home:

1)

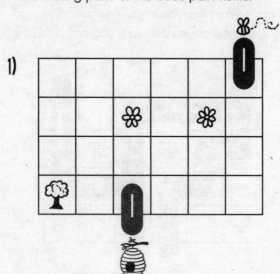

Now turn back and try the second path.

Draw in the missing parts of the bee's path home:

2)

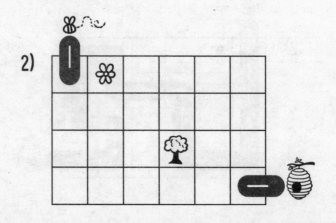

Take a look at the following picture and then, once you think you'll remember it, turn the page.

By picking from the various options below, can you redraw the room exactly as it appeared on the previous page? Once done, compare back to the original picture!

Options:

Take a good look at this list of things you might find in a park, until you think you will remember them. Then, once you're ready, turn the page and follow the instructions.

Duck pond
Playground
Grass
Fountain
Tennis court
Bench
Statue
Flowerbed

The park features are now in a different order, and two have been replaced. Can you circle the two new items?

Cafe

Tennis court

Duck pond

Statue

Flowerbed

Fountain

Grass

Swings

Take a look at this simple picture, then turn the page and see how accurately you can redraw it.

Now try again with the following drawing:

Can you now draw the picture again, exactly as it was shown on the previous page?

Once you've redrawn it, compare back to the picture on the previous page. How close is your version?

Then turn back and try the second task on the previous page. Redraw the picture as accurately as you can, then check back to see how you did.

Have a good look at the following journey through a park, shown by the dashed line. When you're ready, turn the page and see if you can redraw it.

START

?

FINISH

Here's the same park map, but without the route marked! Can you draw it back in?

START

?

FINISH

Some of the squares in this picture have been shaded in. On the next page you'll see the same picture, but all of the squares will be blank so it will be your job to shade them in to match this page. Spend as long as you think you need in order to remember which squares are shaded, then turn the page.

1)

Now do the same with this second pattern:

2)

Shade in the squares to match the picture on the previous page:

1)

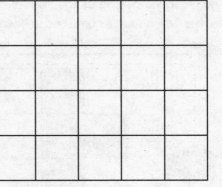

Now turn back and try the second pattern.

Shade in the squares to match the picture on the previous page:

2)

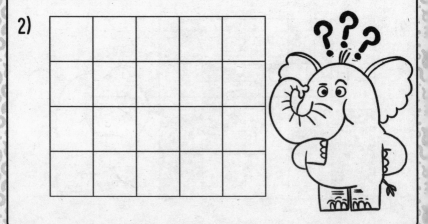

Study this list of passwords and number codes until you think you will remember them all. Then, turn the page and follow the instructions.

Computer login: Pas5w0rd

Bank-card PIN: 1357

Online class login: SchoolNet22

Phone unlock code: 345345

1) Which number code was the longest: the bank-card PIN or the phone unlock code?

....

2) What was the password for the online class login?

....

3) What is the bank-card's PIN code?

....

4) Which of these is the correct password for the computer login?

a) Pa55w0rd

b) p4s5w0rd

c) Pas5w0rd

d) pas5w0Rd

Spend one or two minutes reading the list of facts about the continent of Asia, below. Then, turn the page and see if you can answer the questions.

- The largest country entirely in Asia is China. The capital of China is Beijing.

- The Asian city with the largest population is Tokyo, which is in Japan.

- The Taj Mahal (pictured below) is the name of a famous building in India.

- The largest island in Asia is Borneo, which is shared by three countries.

- More than 4 billion people live in Asia.

1) In what country is the Taj Mahal?

   a) Japan

   b) Mongolia

   c) India

   d) Pakistan

2) Three countries share the largest island in Asia. What is its name?

....

3) What is the name of the capital of China?

....

4) How many people live in Asia, according to the facts on the previous page?

   a) Less than 3 billion

   b) More than 4 billion

   c) At least 6 billion

5) In which country is Tokyo located?

....

Spend a minute or two studying these cats and their names, until you think you have learned them all. Then, turn the page and follow the instructions.

Nibbles

Kat

Mouser

Whiskers

Furry

Cath

Dave

The cats have all moved around. Can you assign the correct name to each cat?

Read these instructions for making still lemonade, and try to remember the series of steps as best you can. Once you think you're ready, turn the page and see if you can recreate the recipe.

Ingredients:

- lemons
- sugar
- water

Instructions:

1) Squeeze the juice of three lemons into a jug

2) Grate the zest (skin) of one of the lemons into the jug

3) Add three large cups of water to the jug

4) Add two tablespoons of sugar to the jug

5) Stir everything with a spoon until the sugar is fully dissolved

6) Add a handful of ice cubes to cool the lemonade

7) Add slices of lemon to the jug for decoration, then serve.

Here is the lemonade recipe again, but this time the numbers have been removed from the instructions and they have been placed in a different order. Can you add the correct number back in for each instruction?

.... Add three large cups of water to the jug

.... Add two tablespoons of sugar to the jug

.... Add a handful of ice cubes to cool the lemonade

.... Add slices of lemon to the jug for decoration, then serve

.... Grate the zest (skin) of one of the lemons into the jug

.... Squeeze the juice of three lemons into a jug

.... Stir everything with a spoon until the sugar is fully dissolved

Take some time to remember the three numbers on the page below, then turn the page and answer the two maths questions. Try to do this without writing down the three numbers again.

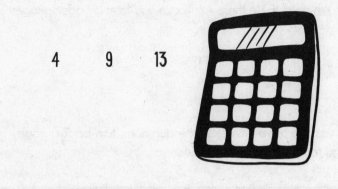

4   9   13

Now try memorizing these four numbers instead, and again then turn the page and answer the questions.

2   4   5   9

1) What number do you get if you add together the two highest values?

....

2) Which of these three totals can you form by adding together any two of the numbers?

   a) 12   b) 16   c) 17

Once you have answered the questions, turn back a page and try the second set of numbers.

---

1) Which of these three totals can you form by adding together any two of the numbers?

   a) 8   b) 9   c) 10

2) What number do you get if you add the lowest and highest numbers?

....

Have a good look at the following picture, and try to remember what it looks like. On the following page the same picture will appear, but with six differences. Once you think you'll remember the picture below well enough to know what's changed, turn the page.

Circle the six differences in the image below:

All
of the
ANSWERS

MEMORY GAME 1

MEMORY GAME 2

Missing sock 1: has stripes.
Missing sock 2: has lightning bolts.

MEMORY GAME 3

Missing face 1:   Missing face 2:

MEMORY GAME 4

The first new entry is: snowboarding.
The second new entry is: basketball.

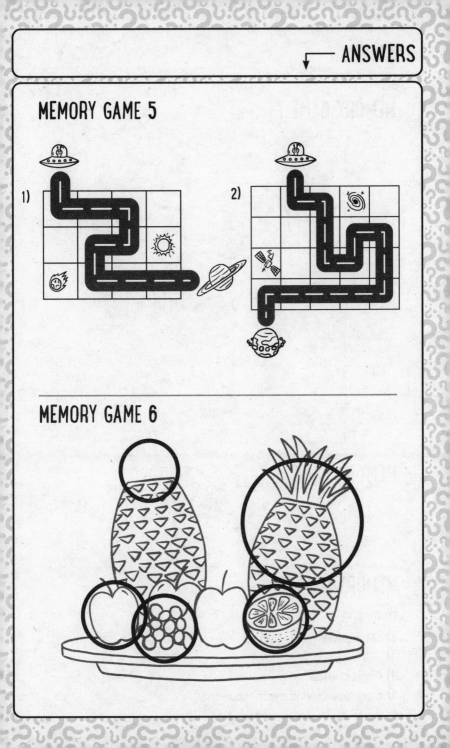

MEMORY GAME 5

1)

2)

MEMORY GAME 6

MEMORY GAME 7

MEMORY GAME 8

MEMORY GAME 9

1) Triceratops
2) Diplodocus
3) Velociraptor
4) Argentinosaurus
5) Stegosaurus and Tyrannosaurus

MEMORY GAME 10

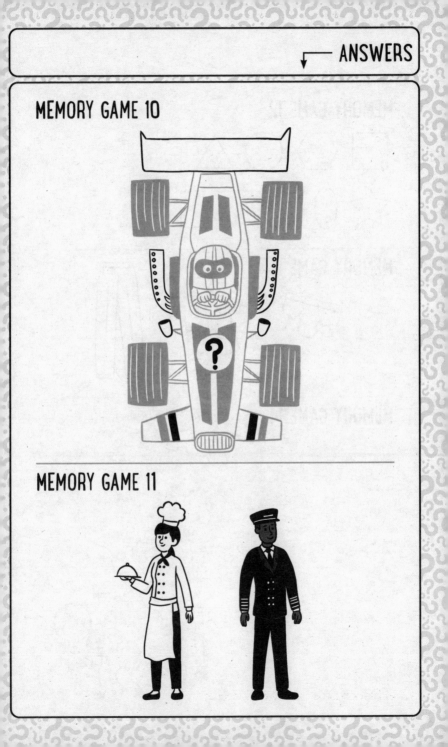

MEMORY GAME 11

MEMORY GAME 12

MEMORY GAME 13

MEMORY GAME 14

MEMORY GAME 15

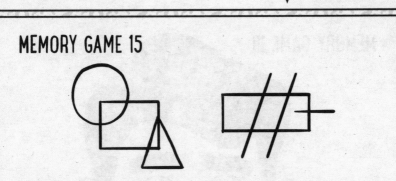

MEMORY GAME 16

Jordan and James have had their names swapped.

MEMORY GAME 17

1) Coins
2) Tiara
3) Sword
4) Pearls
5) Diamonds

1) Gold
2) Skeleton key
3) Rubies
4) Goblet
5) Shield

MEMORY GAME 18

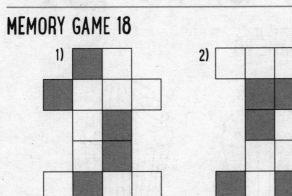

MEMORY GAME 19

MEMORY GAME 20

MEMORY GAME 21

Missing countries:
Portugal
Finland

Missing cities:
Paris
Athens
Rome
Brussels

MEMORY GAME 22

Bananas
Eggs
Milk
Cheese
Pet food
Apples
Magazine
Orange juice

MEMORY GAME 23

Missing from the top:
Guitar
Flute

Missing from the bottom:
Trumpet
Saxophone
Trombone

MEMORY GAME 24

The missing sports are golf and tennis.

MEMORY GAME 25

MEMORY GAME 26

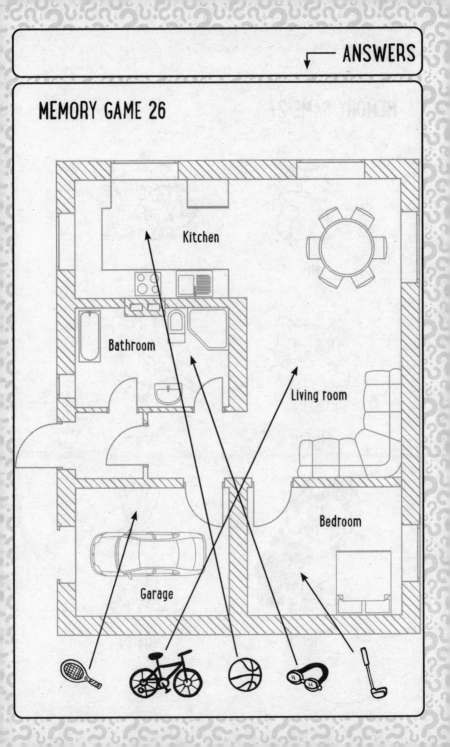

MEMORY GAME 28

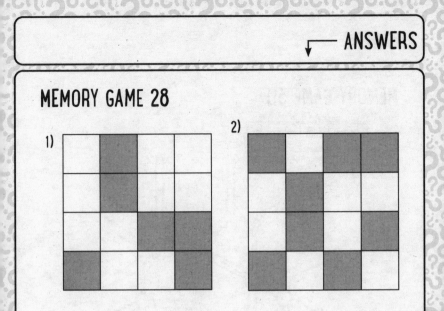

1)
2)

MEMORY GAME 29

The numbers are 2, 4, 6, 7 and 9 - which can be written in any order.

The numbers are 2, 3, 4, 5, 8 and 10 - which can be written in any order.

MEMORY GAME 30

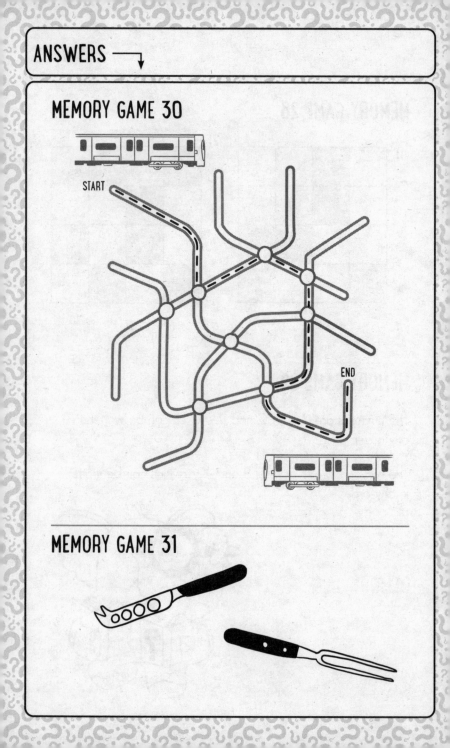

START

END

MEMORY GAME 31

MEMORY GAME 32

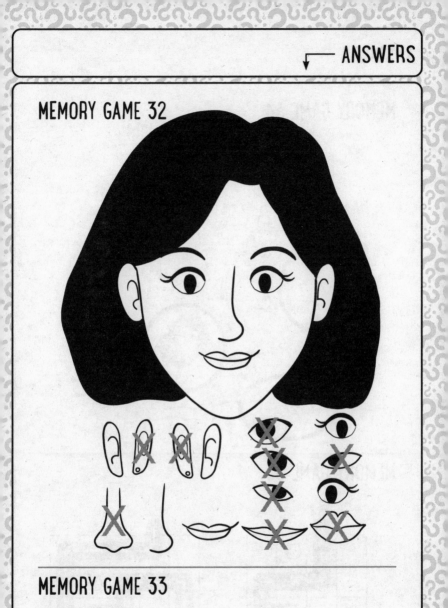

MEMORY GAME 33

1) Tanzania
2) Egypt
3) Kenya
4) Algeria
5) South Africa

ANSWERS →

MEMORY GAME 34

MEMORY GAME 35

1)

2)

MEMORY GAME 36

Aida

Dave

Parky

MEMORY GAME 37

MEMORY GAME 38

The missing items are the phone, wallet and bag.

MEMORY GAME 39

MEMORY GAME 40

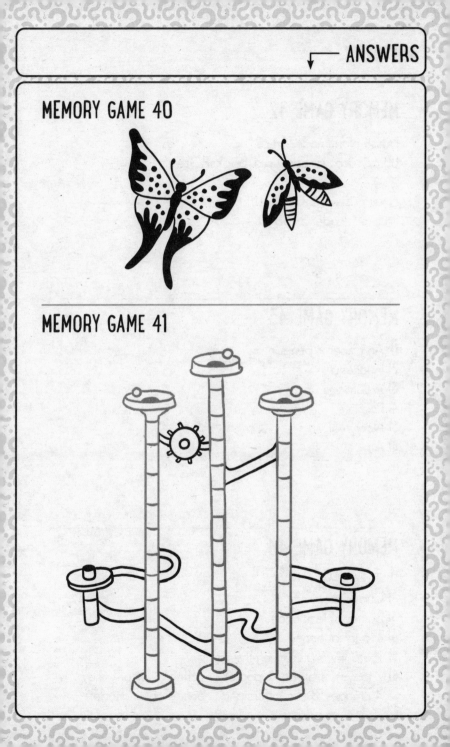

MEMORY GAME 41

MEMORY GAME 42

House alarm code: 1423
Library account password: BooksRGreat

Email password: CoMpUtErPaSs
Bike-lock code: 246810

MEMORY GAME 43

1) An Emperor penguin
2) Indonesia
3) A flamingo
4) Rosettes
5) Nocturnal
6) A blue whale

MEMORY GAME 44

1) 4 oranges
2) Cucumbers
3) Bottles of lemonade
4) c: a jar of honey
5) There were 6 items on the list.
6) 2 loaves of bread, 1 packet of coffee, 1 jar of honey,
   4 oranges, 3 cucumbers and 5 bottles of lemonade.

MEMORY GAME 45

MEMORY GAME 46

DJIBOUTI
LUXEMBOURG
MONACO
SAN MARINO
SINGAPORE
VATICAN CITY

MEMORY GAME 47

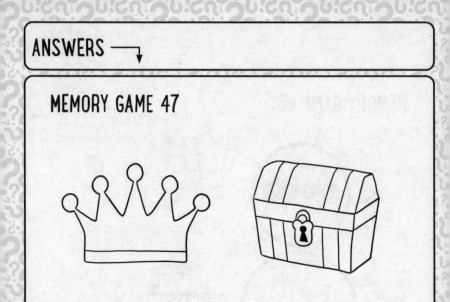

MEMORY GAME 48

1) 13
2) c: 18

1) b: 18
2) 8

MEMORY GAME 49

Missing from the top:
Lion
Lemon

Missing from the bottom:
Lamb
Log
Lizard

MEMORY GAME 50

1) 5
2) d: chop the tomatoes into quarters
3) Mozzarella
4) Give everything a stir
5) Basil leaves
6) Lettuce

MEMORY GAME 51

MEMORY GAME 52

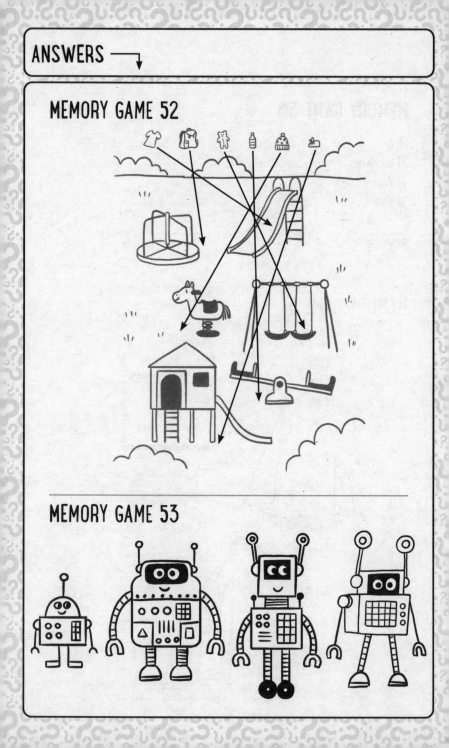

MEMORY GAME 53

MEMORY GAME 54

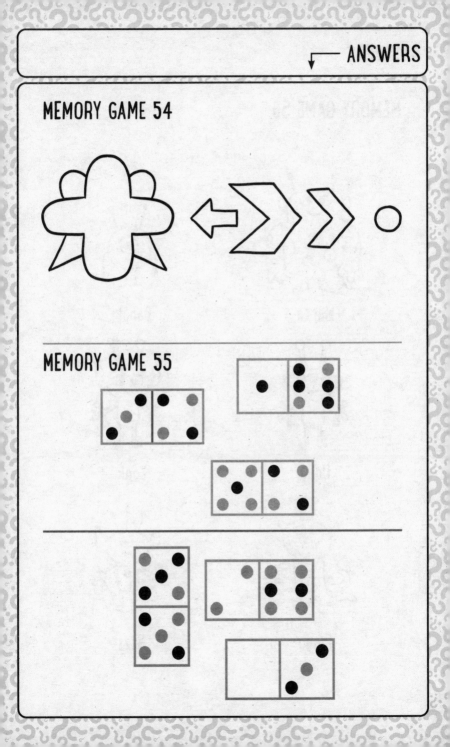

MEMORY GAME 55

MEMORY GAME 56

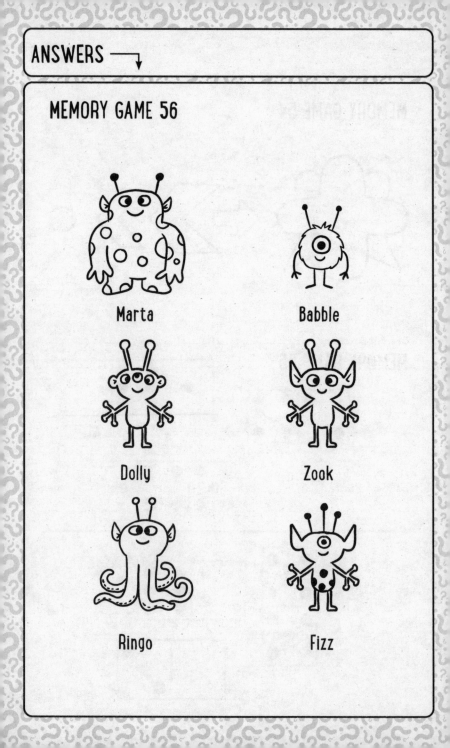

Marta

Babble

Dolly

Zook

Ringo

Fizz

MEMORY GAME 57

MEMORY GAME 58

(6) (2) (1) (3) (4) (5)

(7) (5) (3) (2) (1) (6) (4)

MEMORY GAME 59

1) Nauru
2) c: Bolivia
3) Canberra
4) d: Brasília
5) b: False

MEMORY GAME 60

The four new words are brown (nworB), black (kcalB), brain (niarB) and boat (taoB).

MEMORY GAME 61

MEMORY GAME 62

MEMORY GAME 63

MEMORY GAME 64

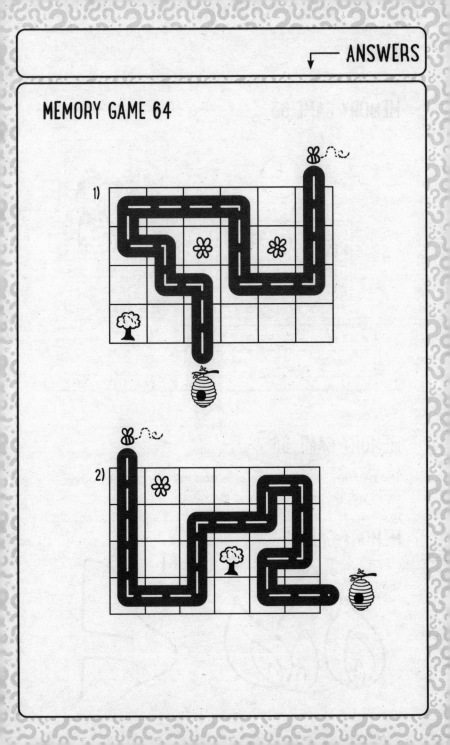

MEMORY GAME 65

MEMORY GAME 66

The two new items are the cafe and the swings. They have replaced the playground and the bench.

MEMORY GAME 67

MEMORY GAME 68

START

FINISH

ANSWERS

MEMORY GAME 69

1)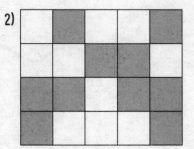
2)

MEMORY GAME 70

1) Phone unlock code
2) SchoolNet22
3) 1357
4) c: Pas5w0rd

MEMORY GAME 71

1) c: India
2) Borneo
3) Beijing
4) b: more than 4 billion
5) Japan

MEMORY GAME 72

Dave

Mouser

Kat

Furry

Cath

Whiskers

Nibbles

MEMORY GAME 73

3) Add three large cups of water to the jug
4) Add two tablespoons of sugar to the jug
6) Add a handful of ice cubes to cool the lemonade
7) Add slices of lemon to the jug for decoration, then serve
2) Grate the zest (skin) of one of the lemons into the jug
1) Squeeze the juice of three lemons into a jug
5) Stir everything with a spoon until the sugar is fully dissolved

MEMORY GAME 74

1) 22
2) c: 17

1) b: 9
2) 11